Joyful SURRENDER

A 40-DAY JOURNEY TO GREATER DEPENDENCE ON JESUS

ROLLAND & HEIDI BAKER

RIVER

PUBLISHING

River Publishing & Media Ltd
info@river-publishing.co.uk

www.river-publishing.co.uk

Scripture quotations are taken from:

New International Version (NIV)

Amplified Bible (AMP)

The Message (MSG)

Cover Photo by Pablo Heimplatz on Unsplash

ISBN 978-1-908393-88-3

Printed in the USA by Versa Press, Inc.

Contents

Day One – Grow Up!   5

Day Two – Trust His Leading   9

Day Three – Ask For The Right Things   13

Day Four – Simple and Uncomplicated   15

Day Five – The Hard Sayings of Jesus   17

Day Six – His Way   21

Day Seven – The Power of Joy   23

Day Eight – Joy and Suffering   25

Day Nine – Everyday Suffering   29

Day Ten – Yes, Papa   31

Day Eleven – Breathe Out   33

Day Twelve – Get a Boat   35

Day Thirteen – Look Forward   41

Day Fourteen – Trust   43

Day Fifteen – Expect the Unexpected   47

Day Sixteen – Be Present   51

Day Seventeen – God's Not Santa Claus   53

Day Eighteen – Beautiful Mercy   57

Day Nineteen – A Love That Never Dies   61

Day Twenty – Promises   63

Day Twenty-One – Overshadowed   65

Day Twenty-Two – Persevere   67

Day Twenty-Three – Shine   73

Day Twenty-Four – Adopted   75

Day Twenty-Five – He Knows You!   77

Day Twenty-Six – The Mind of Christ   81

Day Twenty-Seven – Willing to Die?   83

Day Twenty-Eight – A Powerful Crop   87

Day Twenty-Nine – Finding God   91

Day Thirty – Fire   95

Day Thirty-One – Only Jesus   97

Day Thirty-Two – Cast Your Crown   101

Day Thirty-Three – Delighting   105

Day Thirty-Four – Simple Love   109

Day Thirty-Five – Step by Step   111

Day Thirty-Six – A River Running Through You   115

Day Thirty-Seven – Unquenchable Grace   117

Day Thirty-Eight – Mercy Triumphs   121

Day Thirty-Nine – Godly Power   123

Day Forty – Make God Happy   127

About IRIS Global   129

Day One
Grow Up!

"Let the little children come to me, and do not hinder them, for the Kingdom of God belongs to such as these."

(Mark 10:14)

Many of us fill our lives with endless conferences, Bible school teaching, theology classes and leadership meetings. All of this is great, but these activities have one aim: to fill our brains with more knowledge and information. If we're not careful, we can spend more time learning about *how to mature* than actually doing it!

We know that Jesus teaches in Luke 18:17, "Anyone who does not receive the Kingdom of God like a little child will never enter it." But how do we do that as grown-up, mature adults?

We can't do it by being religious. We can't do it by performing for Him. We do it by simply making Jesus the great pleasure and excitement of our lives – by putting our trust completely in Him.

Do you remember curling up for a cuddle with your mom, dad or grandparents when you were little? Do you remember the safety you felt, not worrying about anything? That is the perfect picture of a mature, grown-up, responsible, strong Christian!

Being utterly dependent on Jesus is not weak or irresponsible – it actually demonstrates a deep, trusting faith in Him. Many of us will have to work to redevelop that kind of faith in Jesus. Or perhaps discover it for the first time.

Have you noticed how children are not at all self-conscious? They express their emotions freely, openly and honestly. They dance, sing or cry without embarrassment. Father God points us to their example. He longs for us to be inspired by their freedom and lack of cynicism. This worries some people – especially in church! They think that any outward demonstration of emotion that might draw attention is fleshly and of the world. So they keep still and quiet. Even as they worship, they can look glum and formal. They won't raise their hands or move their feet, for fear of looking silly... or childish.

But what kind of love do we have if we won't express it?

When we worship, we are demonstrating our delight and love for God with all of our being. The spirit, soul *and body* are all involved. Jesus loves us so much, let's love Him back! Let's worship Him with our whole beings. Let's release our heartfelt love by raising our hands and dancing and shouting. We're not wooden puppets waiting for God to pull our strings.

King David made a complete spectacle of himself dancing with all his might before the Lord. He totally went for it, no holding back. He was so in love with God that he danced like a little child – and Father God loved it!

Be like a child. Worship with all your heart; with your whole self. Don't create a spectacle for the sake of it, but don't worry what others think either. Let yourself go! God can see your heart and He can tell if you're really loving Him. Yell. Dance. Play music. Stand on your head. Sing. Be free.

There's nowhere else in this world where you can be truly free, other than in His presence.

Church should not be the most restrained and controlled moment of your whole week. It should be the free-est!

As Psalm 104:33 says, *"I will sing to the Lord all my life; I will sing praise to my God as long as I live."*

Day Two
Trust His Leading

"'For my thoughts are not your thoughts, neither are your ways my ways,' declares the Lord."

(Isaiah 55:8)

Whenever we think we know what to do, we are in danger. In missions especially, there's a line of reasoning that goes like this...

We want to impact as many people as possible and be the greatest influence we can, so we go about it in a very logical way. First we reach out to the movers and shakers, the rich and famous. We have strategy meetings and do our research. We search out prominent pastors and worship leaders, not wasting our time on the "little" people with no influence, because it will all trickle down to them eventually. We say to ourselves, "Let's plan something BIG!"

What we wouldn't do is start our missions strategy with a "nobody" in the middle of "nowhere". But God doesn't work how we do.

One time we were in Hawaii on our way to Asia. We were in a little church on a sugar plantation in Oahu, spreading the Gospel through dance, drama and theatre. After the meeting, a Filipino lady came up to us and said that we really *must* take our production to the Philippines. Of course, we said this was impossible. We had no ticket, no visas, no money; we didn't know anyone there either.

But she was insistent. She said we had to go and that she would call her brother who lived there. Eventually I gave in and went to the embassy in Honolulu. I told them who we were and what we did, not holding out any hope that we would get a visa to travel. Unbelievably, the whole team got visas in one day! They also changed our plane tickets at no extra cost!

So, we flew off and landed in Manila, not knowing anyone. We had no money at all. No lunch, no hotel, nothing. We just got off the plane with nothing more than the name of this lady's brother.

What we didn't know was that her brother was a famous pilot in the Filipino air force flight demonstration team! Before we knew it, we were all guests of honor at the airbase in Manila and were being hosted by the commanding General of the whole airbase. Soon a meeting had been organized on the airbase for around 5,000, including the pilots and their families and friends. 2,500 people came to the Lord on the first day alone! The General then gave us use of his private jet to fly all over the Philippines.

Recalling this story now, I'm sure you can see it's just ridiculous. Miraculous! We listened to a lady in a tiny church in the middle of nowhere, followed the Spirit's leading, and God opened a door for us to preach all over the Philippines. Only God could do that. But we could easily have missed it.

Challenge yourself to trust God's leading, whether it makes any sense to you or not. Be attentive and listen to His Spirit. Follow His prompts and see what amazing opportunities He might open up for you today.

Day Three
Ask For The Right Things

"Ask and it will be given to you. Seek and you will find. Knock and the door will be opened to you. For everyone who asks receives. He who seeks finds. And to him who knocks, the door will be opened."

(Matthew 7:7)

When holy hunger grips you, you will start asking for things you didn't even know you wanted. When you live a life *fully given* to God, that's when you start asking for the right things.

Psalm 37:4 says, *"Delight yourself also in the Lord and He will give you the desires of your heart."*

The problem is, we often don't know the true desires of our heart. We *think* we do, but God knows better.

What does it mean to "delight" in Him? To delight yourself in the Lord means to dive into Him. To be submerged, swallowed up, and totally surrendered to Him. In the secret place of His presence, in that place of worship, there is a supernatural alignment that takes place, where your heart and His heart connect.

When we are fully connected to God and fully known by Him, there is no fear in trusting Him with our dearest hopes and desires and dreams. And as we make God our love, our life, our all in all, the Holy Spirit floods our hearts. His presence dissolves the hard edges, the hurts, the frozen ground, and makes our hearts more like His.

This is so exciting! You might surprise yourself with a sudden longing to do something or to go somewhere. You will pray for people you don't like and help people who have just been rude to you. You will find yourself choosing to forgive instead of holding onto offense. As our hearts are softened, new desires spring up and, many times, things we thought we wanted fall away.

In that place of adoration, that place of exaltation, that's where you will start thinking of things to ask for. The things that really matter.

Dare you dive in? Dare you offer God your heart?

He loves you so much, you have nothing to fear. Let your desires become His and He will fulfill them.

Day Four
Simple and Uncomplicated

"Love is to be sincere and active..."

Romans 12:9 (AMP)

Have you noticed that our Christian bookstores are full of books on "How to do signs and wonders", "How to experience the miraculous" or "How to get the supernatural working in your life"? Every conference is about "equipping" and "training" – but how much of the New Testament is actually about that? How many Bible verses teach us how to do signs and wonders? None. Zero. Not one verse! Miracles certainly get people's attention, but what happens after that? Satanists and witch doctors can perform miracles too, but where do they lead?

Our greatest weapon is not supernatural signs and wonders. It's fearless love that's going to touch people. When we simply carry the presence of Jesus everywhere we go, others will feel it. In Africa, we have a saying we repeat all the time, "God is good, God is good, God is good!" We say it because we know that's what is going to win through. When the world is filled with terror, we should radiate peace. When others turn away, we should open our arms wide. It's so easy. Love is the answer to every issue in life.

The well-known verses of 1 Corinthians 13 say, *"Love is patient, love is kind. It does not envy, it does not boast, it is not proud. It does not dishonor others, it is not self-seeking, it is not easily angered, it keeps no record of wrongs. Love does not delight in evil but rejoices in the truth. It always protects, always trusts, always hopes, always perseveres. Love never fails."*

Love is preeminent. Our faith is not a complicated, theological puzzle we have to fathom out. It is simple. It's easy.

Throughout your day, whatever happens, always come back to love. Anchor yourself in love. Let the love of Christ determine how you react, what you say and what you do.

When you are tempted to react, pause and ask yourself, "What would Love do?" because Jesus is the perfect embodiment of love.

Jesus hung out with the lost, the unloved, the rejected. Why would He do that? Because of love. Deep down we all want to be loved, to be noticed, to be valued. The smallest gesture can transform someone's life. That extra kindness. The listening ear. The compassion. A hug.

Jesus said in Matthew 15:14-16, *"You are the light of the world ... let your light shine before others, that they may see your good deeds and glorify your Father in heaven."*

Be brave. Let the fire of God's love burn so brightly that the world sees it and is dazzled.

Day Five
The Hard Sayings of Jesus

"A wise son heeds and accepts (and is the result of) his father's discipline and instruction."

(Proverbs 13:1 AMP)

A lot of people talk about the "hard sayings of Jesus" as though they are a "toxic" element of the Gospel that we need to be shielded from. They think we should play down these sayings because it will make the Gospel unpalatable. Better to hide these sayings away, or just never mention them at all!

Many things Jesus said were extremely challenging. Matthew 19:21 says, *"If you want to be perfect, go, sell your possessions and give to the poor."* In Matthew 10:38 He says, *"Whoever does not take up their cross and follow me is not worthy of me."* It's easy to think, *that's not for me. It's too hard.* We want an easier Gospel, so we look for a church that makes us feel good about ourselves; a place where we can make friends and have fun.

"Let's just clean the Bible up a bit," we say. "If we get rid of all the negative stuff and focus on the good bits, it will be more appealing to the world!"

By doing this we create a bigger problem. Life isn't like that. We shouldn't make out that everything is great when you become a Christian, or that God doesn't have tough stuff to teach us. Each of us goes through hard times. We are all challenged by events in our lives. Pretending that in Christ we won't be challenged like this is dangerous. Preaching a Gospel of ease and prosperity forces those who are genuinely struggling to withdraw. They feel ashamed and embarrassed by their lives. They think something must be badly wrong or that God is not pleased with them.

That is not true.

If we want to know God intimately, we need to know the full picture. We have to embrace all He has to say – even the hard parts. Every verse in Scripture exists for a reason, so we need to ask ourselves, "Why is that verse there? What truth is God trying to teach me?"

God disciplines us, guides us, and teaches us because we are His children and He loves us. He uses *every* verse of the Bible to do that.

As 2 Timothy 3:16 confirms, *"All Scripture is God-breathed and is useful for teaching, rebuking, correcting and training in righteousness."*

When you next experience a hard time in your life, don't shrink back from God. Turn to Him. Humble yourself and let Him guide you. Open yourself up to His wisdom. Likewise, if you know someone else who is in a "hard place" right now, don't judge them. Come alongside them. Point them to Jesus and help them experience His love.

Remember that the hard sayings of Jesus are not restrictions. With God's wisdom, they can be open doors to freedom, joy and life.

Day Six
His Way

"For I know the plans I have for you, declares the Lord, plans to prosper you and not to harm you, plans to give you a hope and a future."

(Jeremiah 29:11)

We love to be in charge of our lives, don't we? When we dream about our futures, how many of us think we know better than God? We have our own plans and ideas, and the unsettling worry is that if we invite God into the equation, He will take it all away. Or make us do something we hate. We think it will mean giving up every hope and desire to trudge along a miserable "Christian" path. But nothing could be further from the truth!

Trusting God is not slavery. It's not being a robot.

Psalm 37:4 says, *"Take delight in the Lord, and He will give you the desires of your heart."*

We all make plans, but when we take a step of faith and ask God to be involved in those plans, we can rest in the knowledge that His way is the best way.

We also read in Proverbs 3:5, *"Trust in the Lord with all your heart and lean not on your own understanding; in all your ways acknowledge Him, and He will make your paths straight."*

Being led by the Spirit is not being stuck in religion.

It's not having everything we value taken away from us. It's the absolute opposite. It is where we find true peace, joy, freedom, love, purity and a flow of wisdom.

In fact, when the Holy Spirit is most in control of us, that is when we are *most* free, and *truly* alive. That is so cool. Isn't it wonderful that we have a Father God who knows us so well – our different gifts, our personalities – that He knows perfectly what we need to make us happy?

He is the life, the living water, the source. When you plan your day, or make decisions, never be tempted to "lean on your own understanding". Always trust Holy Spirit and follow where He leads.

Day Seven
The Power of Joy

"The joy of the Lord is your strength."

(Nehemiah 8:10)

Many people walk around as if they have all the cares of the world on their shoulders. They have no joy, no energy and no enthusiasm. They grumble and complain. Life seems to be one big, disappointing struggle.

It shouldn't be like that!

Do you know that *joy* is actually a God-given power source?

Nehemiah 8:10 gives us a simple equation: the *joy of the Lord = strength.*

If we find ourselves weary and needing more strength, what we actually need is more joy!

If we live solely for ourselves, going our own way, then we become dead inside. But when we live connected to God and fully yielded to Him, we have a supernatural energy source of joy and life that wells up inside, like a river of living water.

Joy is powerful.

I learnt from the persecuted Church in China that joy is the energy of the Holy Spirit. It keeps us steady when things get rough. It brings excitement, passion, hope. It is also our greatest weapon. It gives us the ability to laugh in Satan's face when he tries to steal our faith and defeat us. The joy of the Lord is unshakable. It's pure and powerful.

Psalm 16:11 says, *"You make known to me the paths of life; you will fill me with joy in your presence, with eternal pleasures at your right hand."*

If life seems like an ordeal, connect yourself to the power source. As you walk with Jesus, realize that you have the power of the resurrected Son of God living within you. Be joyful by faith. Draw on His power when you least feel like it. Make a commitment to walk not just in faith and love, but with real *joy*.

Day Eight
Joy and Suffering

"So do not fear, for I am with you; do not be dismayed, for I am your God. I will strengthen you and help you; I will uphold you with my righteous right hand."

(Isaiah 41:10)

In our book *Always Enough*, we wrote about a vision Heidi had of the thousands of kids she was supposed to take care of. At the time we were struggling to look after a few hundred and it was overwhelming. Heidi's natural response was, "No! I can't take care of so many!" Telling her to look into His eyes, Jesus responded, "Because I died, there will always be enough." Then He handed her a cup and said it was a cup of both joy and suffering.

"Will you drink it?" He said.

The truth is, the Christian life is made up of both joy and suffering. The question is: *will you drink it?*

The modern Church is quick to eliminate the idea of suffering. Many teach that because Jesus suffered, you won't have to. But this leads to the idea is that if anyone is suffering in the Church it is because they're not exercising their faith, not praying enough, or they don't know who they are, as children of the King on this earth.

Let's think about this for a minute. Suffering is not something that happens to just a few specific people, chosen by God for that single, special purpose. The Bible is *filled* with people whose lives were a mixture of both suffering and joy. The apostles were beaten, broken, abused, shipwrecked, yet praising the Lord and spreading the good news of His love. How can we think that it would be different for us?

It would have been impossible for us to have survived in Mozambique if we hadn't learnt that the Christian life is a cup of both joy and suffering. The people we've met, the places we've visited, the terrible situations we've faced, have all brought a mixture of joy and hardship into our lives. However, it is not the experience of suffering that really matters, but how we react to it.

Do we turn away from God? Or look to Him? Are we prepared to let Him take our hand and guide us through each situation? Or do we fight Him and become bitter and angry? Each hardship, each moment of suffering, is an opportunity to draw closer to God. In times of suffering we need to seek His will and wisdom *more* wholeheartedly. Through this our character, strength, compassion, resilience and wisdom will grow.

Paul prays in Ephesians 1:17, "*I keep asking that the God of our Lord Jesus Christ, the glorious Father, may give you the Spirit of wisdom and revelation, so that you may know Him better.*"

Every day let's seek to "know Him better". Whether we are in a time of joy or suffering, let's take God's hand and walk with

Him through it, knowing that, *"The Lord is good to those whose hope is in Him, to the one who seeks Him"* (Lamentations 3:25).

Day Nine
Everyday Suffering

"For if you forgive other people when they sin against you, your heavenly Father will also forgive you."

(Matthew 6:14-15)

Question: How do you know when you are walking in the supernatural, *agape* love, that only God has?

Answer: When it is tested. And the fact is, it is tested every single day.

Many of us think of "suffering" as being locked up in solitary confinement for twenty years. Or being jailed for our faith; or shot; or beheaded for being a Christian.

I'm not talking about that. I'm talking about everyday suffering. The kind of suffering that occurs when somebody disappoints you or hurts you. When they gossip about you or are cruel. The normal reaction is to get upset. Maybe we confront the person? Or argue and retaliate? Some of us hold grudges for years, laying the blame squarely at the other person's feet. In church we have more than enough opportunities to do this! How many churches do you know that have split because of one person turning against another? People jostle for position, they gossip and slander each other. Perhaps the pastor did something bad and you're really angry about it. You think you have a right to be too, so you talk about it with others, then you pray to God and ask Him to "fix" that person. Sound familiar?

As soon as you get angry, you're no use to God. As soon as you get irritated or impatient, you've taken offense. When you feel sorry for yourself, or complain, or gossip, then you've lost the victory. Because if you don't turn your cheek, if you don't go the second mile, if you don't forgive, if you don't love your enemy, then you're not truly walking in love.

These are the everyday hardships the Bible talks about. Which makes every day an opportunity for us to learn and grow.

Ephesians 4:31-32 says very clearly, *"Get rid of all bitterness, rage and anger, brawling and slander, along with every form of malice. Be kind and compassionate to one another, forgiving each other, just as in Christ God forgave you."*

The next time your love is tested… Stop!

Choose to react in love. Try to bless those who hurt you. Try to understand them. Keep finding out what it means to love people, no matter how they treat you. This is a form of suffering that will bring us freedom and peace, and through which we are daily transformed.

Day Ten
Yes, Papa

*"For my thoughts are not your thoughts, neither are your ways
my ways."*

(Isaiah 55:8)

None of us are too clever or too extraordinary that we don't
need God's help. We all need help. I need help! I want to help a
dying world, but I can't do it on my own. I need to know God's
plans and follow His way. I need to empty myself out so that
He can fill me. I need to say, "Here's my life, Lord. Let me wear
the turban of Your thoughts. Let me be so fully possessed by
You that even my mind is captured by You."

On March 14th 1976, I met Jesus. I was so desperate for God,
I simply said, "Take me. Fill me. Use me." In all the years that
have followed I have come back to the same realization over
and again: *I can't do anything for the Lord on my own.*

When I arrived in Mozambique, I prayed the same prayer.
Since then, several times each day, I prostrate myself before the
Lord and ask for His help. And He comes in magnificent ways.

In Matthew 19:26 we read, *"Jesus looked at them and said, 'With man this is impossible, but with God all things are possible.'"*

How on earth would I be able to reach the lost, or look after thousands of children without His help? Just handing out a Jesus-flyer and saying, "Here sweetie, read this" isn't going to do it. I need God's ideas and His unique strategies.

Try it for yourself.

Pray for help. Pray for answers. How do I reach the lost in my town? How do I help the homeless? Without Him, all our efforts will come to nothing. But with Him, a city can be shaken. And it just takes one person who will humbly say,

"Take me. Fill me. Use me."

Ask Him to fill you with His love; the kind of love that compels you to offer yourself totally and completely each and every day.

Pray this with me now: "Take me. Possess me. Fill me. Use me. Do anything you like with me." And when He offers to help, which He always will, just say "Yes, Papa!"

Day Eleven
Breathe Out

"And to know the love that surpasses all knowledge—that you may be filled to the measure of all the fullness of God."

(Ephesians 3:19)

One day I was lying before the Lord and I heard His voice so clearly. He said, "The river flows in the low places."

What He was saying to me was: in order to be fully covered by the river of His power and love, you need to get as low as you can go. You need to hold your breath and dive in.

Then once you are under... Breathe out.

Surrender. Give Him everything. Let it all go. Trust Him.

He will carry you on His wonderful currents, He will toss you on His waves. And do you know, there's no limit? "The measure of all the fullness" means just that – it is a never-ending flow. You can have as much of God as you would like. Isn't that wild?

But what if the thought of letting go scares you? What if you think that giving everything up for God makes you some kind of doormat or a puppet? Look at this verse in John 10:10. Jesus said,

"I have come that they might have life and life to the full."

"Life to the full" is a wonderful promise, isn't it? But it comes through our total surrender to the One who truly loves us. Think about Jesus. He is the King of glory but, out of love for us, He was born here on this earth, naked, as a baby. He fully yielded Himself to the Father and now He is asking us to do the same. But we cannot do it in our own strength and we're not left on our own. We have the Holy Spirit. He will teach us, guide us, fill us, and help us in every way.

Say with me, "Fill me Holy Spirit. Take me into the deep river of Your love."

Just yield. Try it. Walk into the river and dive under. Yield yourself to God. It will shock you to find out just what He can do through your little life!

Day Twelve
Get a Boat

"He will not be disheartened or crushed; He will persevere until He has established justice on the earth; And the coastlands will wait expectantly for His law."

Isaiah 42:4 (AMP)

When I was in Mozambique, I wanted to reach a tribe called the Macau. They were far away and all the missionaries I spoke to told me I couldn't do it. They said they had tried and failed and they made sure I knew all of the reasons why it was impossible!

But you see, you can do anything if God has asked you to do it. If you get low enough, full enough, you can do anything. Because it's by His power, not yours.

We set off. Rolland flew us out to the tribe. I said to him, "Fly low. Really, really low." We swooped down so low that I could feel the water spray on my fingers and I started looking at village after village. I noticed that they had no roads, no landing strip – they were just little tiny villages along the side of the ocean. I said to God, "How do I get there? What do I do?" I was sobbing because I knew how much Jesus loved these people.

And God said, "Get a boat."

You would think that was easy. At first, I got a kayak, but I couldn't reach the villages because it was too hard to row and I got too tired. Then I tried a speedboat, but the men who were going to help me were thieves and never delivered the boat. I called everyone I knew and I tried everything.

But, if God puts something in your heart, you have to finish it. You can't give up the moment a thing becomes difficult. If you have a vision, you need to press through the difficulties and ask for God's help.

Galatians 6:9 says, *"Let us not grow weary in doing good, for at the proper time we will reap a harvest if we do not give up."*

I said to God, "I know the kayak didn't work. The speedboat didn't work either. Now what?"

Finally, I was promised a boat from Canada, but was told we would have to pay a 70% import duty to get it to Mozambique. I didn't care what it cost, I wanted to see those tribes come to Jesus, so we paid the tax. I was so full of God's heart for those people that I *had* to go.

We hired a truck to get the boat. Then, as we crossed the border, an accident caused a crack in the boat's motor. I thought, "Somebody must be able to fix a boat!"

It took exactly 2 years, 7 months and 10 days to get a boat that could reach the Macau, but eventually we had it and we went.

What has God asked *you* to do? What has God put in *your* heart?

Think about this: if God has called you to speak to someone, or do something, and the first time you do it, they spit at you or hurl abuse, what do you do? Do you give up? No! You lay down and let the Holy Spirit crash over you. Then you do it again, and again, and again…

What has God asked
you to do that you are
holding back from? What
are you not surrendering
to Him out of fear of
the unknown, or an
unwillingness to step out?

Do you know His power
is perfected in our
weakness?

Do you know He longs to
help you?

Day Thirteen
Look Forward

"He made known to us the mystery of His will according to His good pleasure, which He purposed in Christ."

(Ephesians 1:9 AMP)

Do you know that God has a plan and will for your life? Do you want His will? If so, you must look forward.

Ephesians 1:5 (AMP) says, *"He predestined and lovingly planned for us to be adopted to Himself as children through Jesus Christ, in accordance with the kind intention and good pleasure of His will."*

You can have 100% confidence that God, who is alive, wants to speak to you and lead you in the mystery of His will. The way He leads and guides is by His heart inside of you – His Spirit whispering to your spirit.

That's your compass! That's what you must follow, despite what the circumstances may look like. Just do what He says! Don't let your compass get broken. Don't go off track. Whether you're a surgeon, a teacher, a gardener or a bus driver, keep

Him front and center in your life. Take every thought and action and submit them before Him.

Ask for wisdom and when He speaks, do what He says! Don't stay trapped somewhere because it's comfortable. And never tell God why something won't work, or why He shouldn't move you on! It's the greatest joy to be in the will of God! Especially don't worry if you think you can't do it. God often puts ideas and callings into us that make no sense *at all* in the natural! But I have a saying:

I can't, but You can, so we will.

Today is the day! Step into your true identity. Step into your destiny, because your destiny is magnificent. He will take your hand and help you understand who you really are. You can do it! You're a new creation, set free by the blood of the Lamb. Stop looking backward in the rearview mirror – everything you've done in the past is gone. Whatever you did, if you've repented of it, *it's gone*… sexual sin, stealing, strife, even murder…

You think the sledgehammer of Heaven is falling on you. But do you know where it's hitting? Your rearview mirror!

"Therefore, if anyone is in Christ, the new creation has come: the old has gone, the new is here." (2 Corinthians 5:17)

Take this moment to look forward. God is giving you the strength to do it. Believe the blood of Jesus actually *is* the blood of Jesus and follow the compass into your true identity and calling.

Day Fourteen
Trust

"And He called a little child to him, and placed the child among them. And He said, 'Truly I tell you, unless you change and become like little children, you will never enter the kingdom of heaven. Therefore, whoever takes the lowly position of this child is the greatest in the kingdom of heaven."

(Matthew 18:2)

If you have children, godchildren or friends with kids, then you are blessed with little teachers. The little people around us can teach us a lot about the kingdom of God. If we really want the kingdom of God to break out in our lives, we must become childlike – utterly dependent on Father. We will achieve things of eternal value when we hold onto Papa's hand and say, "I can't do it unless you do it through me. Help me! Lead me!"

What does it mean to be childlike? It means we don't have to worry. Neither do we have to analyze everything. Some people want reasons for everything; they want some kind of proof before they do anything. Children don't do that. They just play and have fun. They don't sit about, wracking their brains, trying to decide whether or not they should play in the yard, or what they should say to the child next to them. They go with the flow!

Philippians 4:6 (AMP) says, *"Do not be anxious or worried about anything..."* This is radical teaching from Paul. In other words, in the Kingdom, you are *not allowed* to worry. Try it. Don't worry about *anything*. It's hard on your own, but when you're trusting God, as a child would their parent, it's possible. Philippians 4:7 continues by saying that *if* we're not anxious, and *if*, in every circumstance and situation, we make our requests known to God, then, *"...the peace of God (that peace which reassures the heart, that peace) which transcends all understanding... is yours."*

Isn't that wonderful? So, what stops us?

We do! With all our theology and religious beliefs, we make God so complex that we think no one can understand Him or draw close to Him. Instead of viewing Him as a loving Father, He is often portrayed as a scary, unapproachable God with strict doctrines that need to be understood and followed. This isn't true.

We think we can please God by what we can do for Him, but let me tell you: there are two sure ways of stopping any move of the Spirit. The first is to get serious. The second is to get organized! Trying to second guess God and turn what He does into a formula has stopped every revival in history. Nowadays the Church has sixty-seven manuals on how to do an outreach and ninety-four on how to pray for people after a meeting. We're the ones making up all the rules. We have turned the Christian life into a recipe, a procedure. But like a little child who thinks they know better than their parent, the minute we think we know what we're doing, we're finished.

This scripture should be our benchmark: *"Trust in the Lord with all your heart and lean not on your own understanding"* (Proverbs 3:5).

Let's humble ourselves and choose to simply depend on God, our Papa. He will show us what to do and teach us how to do it. He is in control and our job is to simply love Him and do what He says.

Day Fifteen
Expect the Unexpected

"In their hearts, humans plan their course, but the Lord establishes their steps."

(Proverbs 16:9)

When I was in my twenties, I felt like my calling was to preach to the multitudes, so Rolland and I took off to Asia. We preached to many thousands of people every night and I loved it. I was dancing, acting and preaching. It was exhilarating, and many came to the Lord. Then one day, out of the blue, I heard a voice say, "Stop!"

Immediately, I rebuked it.

"I rebuke you, Satan, in the name of Jesus!" I yelled.

The voice spoke again.

"Stop!"

And I said again, "No! I rebuke you Satan!"

Then a third time, I heard the voice say, "Stop!"

I realized it was actually Jesus and I was so upset with myself! I started saying sorry, then began to tell Him about all the people I was bringing into His kingdom. But He said to me, "You know nothing about my Kingdom. I want you to sit with the poor."

That was unexpected!

We left the big preaching events and went to find the worst slum in the worst area, and moved in. There was no electricity, no lighting, and we had to climb up dark, smoke-filled stairwells, past gangs and prostitutes.

Every day I went out and sat on the street corner with the poor. They became my teachers. I did this for eighteen years and they taught me a lot about the Kingdom of God. How? They were always desperate; they couldn't think of a plan to fix their lives; and they knew they needed help.

Then God said another unexpected thing. He told me, "The Kingdom belongs to the children. I want you to take all the children home." I was shocked.

"God, I don't do children!" I told Him. I'd never taught Sunday school. I'd never led a kids' meeting. "I'm not the right person for this job!" I protested.

Jesus replied, "You are now. Take the children home because they're going to teach you about the Kingdom of God."

So, I did it. Do you know what? The children became my teachers. Because of what I learned from the poor and the children, the Kingdom of God started breaking out in ways I had never experienced before in my life. Isn't that radical?

What has God asked you to do that you are holding back from? What are you not surrendering to Him out of fear of the unknown, or an unwillingness to step out? Do you know His power is perfected in our weakness? Do you know He longs to help you?

Isaiah 41:10 commands us: *"So do not fear, for I am with you; do not be dismayed for I am your God. I will strengthen you and help you; I will uphold you with my righteous right hand."*

Pray with me. "Crash in on me, Holy Spirit. Help me! I don't have the love. I don't even have the ability or skills, to do the things you're asking me to do. But You do. I trust you, Lord."

Day Sixteen
Be Present

"The Lord is near to all who call upon Him, to all who call on Him in truth."

(Psalm 145:18)

When you live in the secret place, tucked in close to the pounding heart of God, you are ready for anything. It's like you're a sprinter, waiting on the starting line. Nothing phases you, nothing throws you, nothing is impossible – because you are present with God.

When we worship Him, we open our hearts and minds to His Spirit and there is an exchange of His heart and our heart, His thoughts and our thoughts. He guides us, gives us ideas, and shows us things we have never even thought of.

But we have to be present.

Some people struggle with being present in worship. They think, "Oh man, it's been nearly an hour and we haven't had any teaching yet." Their minds wander to what they're going to eat later. Or how they need to catch that person on the way out. They think, "We're wasting time here."

And the fact is, they're right.

If we're not engaged, it *is* a complete waste of time.

Worship is something we do with our hearts and lives, it's not something we listen to. The Holy Spirit knows when we're distracted or bored. He's absolutely not fooled. Even if we're there with our eyes closed, arms in the air, singing the words, He knows where our hearts are at.

He wants us, He loves us. He wants to refresh and fill our hearts and minds with secrets that only He knows. He wants to give us amazing words; answers to problems; strategies from heaven that will channel our lives every day into the glory of God. But He can't if we're not present, if we're not even listening, if we're just playing at church and are not truly hungry and thirsty for Him.

Lift Him up in adoration. Bless Him with Holy Spirit songs. Even if you are exhausted, as you connect with God, a supernatural energy will lift your spirit. If you are troubled, sick or depressed, Daddy God will comfort you and help you.

Rest your head on His chest and listen to His heartbeat.

James 4:8 says, *"Come close to God and He will come close to you."*

In the midst of everything and anything, if we press in close, fully present, He will meet us.

Day Seventeen
God's Not Santa Claus

"You actually believe you can just ask God for anything and He'll give it to you? God's not Santa Claus, you know!"

A theologian once said this to me when I was studying in Oxford, and it came back to me when I thought of this story.

I have seen lots of miracles in my work as a missionary. I have experienced most of the things described in the New Testament, even seeing the dead raised! It's really exciting. Because of this, I thought I had a good understanding of the supernatural, but one day, God shook me up and showed me that I had made Him small in my own eyes. I had put Him in a box and decided what He can and can't do, according to my own expectations and experience.

One day I was in Zimpeto, Mozambique, and it was Christmas. I love Christmas! I love giving gifts and celebrating. We had lots of presents and we invited everybody – the poor, the crippled, the blind, the prostitutes and the street children.

At the party there was a queue of little girls waiting for a present and I said to one, "What do you want sweetheart?" We had hardly anything left but I wanted to give each person a gift.

The little girl looked up and said, "I want beads." The little girl behind her said, "I want beads too," and the one behind her the same. Beads? We had no beads!

The lady next to me hollered, "There's stuffed dogs in the bag."

"There's what?"

"Stuffed dogs – in the bag."

I realized she was telling me that there were some old, dirty, stuffed toys in a garbage bag. I looked back at the little girl.

"I want beads," she whispered.

Well we didn't have any beads.

It was one of those moments where your heart and your head battle with each other. My head wanted to say, "I'm so sorry, I'll buy beads tomorrow, but right now there's only stuffed dogs." But my heart understood God and His heart. My heart knew that God loves us and wants to give us more than we can hope for or imagine. He's not here to give us "stuffed dogs in the bag"! He's not here to give us left-overs. He's here to give us all of Himself.

So, I said to the lady, "They don't want those dogs. They want beads."

I looked into the child's eyes and suddenly the lady reached into the bag and pulled out *beads*! Halleluiah! That absolutely blew my mind.

I didn't think I had put God in a box. But I discovered that even though the box I had put Him in was really big, it was still a box.

Hold your hand out and look at it. What do you think is more complicated to make? Beads or your hand? You are made in the image of God. You are precious to Him. If God can handle beads, can you believe that God can heal your sickness? Guide your life? Provide for you?

Have you squashed God into a tiny box to fit your expectations? Don't do that!

"For with God nothing (is or ever) shall be impossible." (Luke 1:37 AMP)

That theologian was right. God's not Santa Claus. He's much, much better!

Day Eighteen
Beautiful Mercy

"Jesus said, 'Let the little children come to me, and do not hinder them, for the Kingdom of heaven belongs to such as these.'"

(Matthew 19:14)

As a missionary and a student, I have sat under some of the most famous theologians on the planet. I appreciate their understanding of the Word of God, I appreciate their discipline, and I appreciate their intellects. But do you know what? I have learnt my greatest lessons from children and the poor. I call them my heroes.

Jesus said in Matthew 5:3, *"Blessed are the poor in spirit for theirs is the Kingdom of Heaven."*

Over the years, I have found so many little children in Mozambique who have been through so much, and yet reflect Jesus' grace so wonderfully. One girl in particular – I'll call her Sarah – taught me about life, love, forgiveness and mercy. Sarah's mother was a prostitute. She had a sister, also called Sarah (they had different fathers, but their mother gave the two girls the same name!) When I met her, Sarah was a picture of mourning. She was completely miserable. I found her on a garbage heap, dying of starvation and rescued her, but she used to spit, bite, hit me, throw things and steal.

You could be forgiven for asking, *how could that girl teach you anything about the Kingdom of God?!*

She taught me through watching her be transformed as she finally got a hold of love. Everything changed. This girl had been raped and mistreated her whole life; she was full of darkness. But when the light of God came into her, she started pouring out beauty and mercy to everyone around her. Astonishingly, whenever I was sad or tired, or discouraged, she would wrap her little arms around me and give *me* comfort! She *became* comfort.

Jesus said, *"Blessed are those who mourn, for they will be comforted"* (Matthew 5:4).

This is how it works! The Kingdom of God looks like *you,* fully surrendered, taking on the characteristics of a child fully yielded to God.

The Kingdom of God looks like *you,* fully dependent on the One who is totally dependable, carrying the beauty of the Master to someone who is in pain, grieving or lost.

I learnt from Sarah that if you allow God to take you from your place of mourning into the place of His comfort, you will become a comforter to others.

Recently, I watched her stand on the back of a flatbed truck, surrounded by an aggressive crowd who were throwing rocks. She stood there and shouted,

"I'm not afraid of you! I know who I am. Jesus loves you. I used to be dying, but now I'm alive!"

This little girl was full of the power of God and she preached to those people. Do you know what? The crowd listened.

Let her example teach and encourage you too. Yield yourself to God and let His love transform you. You will become a messenger of hope, a bringer of comfort, carrying the presence of the mighty God to the sad and lost.

Day Nineteen
A Love That Never Dies

"A friend loves at all times."

(Proverbs 17:17)

How many of us are suffering because of broken relationships? Whether it's family relationships, friends, at church or in the workplace, the pain is heartbreaking. Often, deep emotional anguish can lead to real, physical sickness. Proverbs 17:22 puts it like this:

"A cheerful heart is good medicine, but a crushed spirit dries up the bones."

We face many crises at Iris Global, but a surprising number of them are rooted in people just not loving each other. That's hard to understand, isn't it? People not being kind or nice to one another.

People will rush to the altar to get healed, or if they are desperate for money, or a job. But who rushes to the altar to become kinder? To stop gossiping and holding grudges? To ask for a deeper love for one another?

Yet the Bible says in John 13:34, *"A new command I give you: Love one another. As I have loved you, so you must love one another."*

That's not a suggestion.

How do we become more loving? It's not simply by praying to Jesus. I know people who've talked to Jesus all their lives and they're rotten! The trick is to do exactly what the Bible says.

Matthew 11:28-30 instructs us, *"Come to me, all you who are weary and burdened, and I will give you rest. Take my yoke upon you and learn from me, for I am gentle and humble in heart, and you will find rest for your souls."*

Jesus simply asks that we come as we are and allow Him to wash us clean that we might be filled with Him. As we go deeper into God's love, we become lesser and Jesus becomes greater within us. In the dwelling place of the Holy Spirit there is no room for pride, offense or hatred. There is only room for *"love, joy, peace, patience, kindness, goodness, faithfulness, gentleness and self-control"* (Galatians 5:22-23).

It is *His* love that transforms us; *His* heart that beats within us.

"We love because He first loved us." (1 John 4:19)

Love is the answer. Press into His presence and open your heart to Him. It's not a matter of trying to get God's power to work for you. Surrender to Him and His ways and you will see supernatural changes occur as His love flows out through you. It's miraculous! And the best bit of all: peace will follow.

"Whatever you have learned or received or heard from me, or seen in me—put it into practice. And the God of peace will be with you." (Philippians 4:9)

Day Twenty
Promises

"You did not choose me but I chose you and appointed you so that you might go and bear fruit."

(John 15:16)

Do you have promises from God? Have they all come to pass? Mine haven't. There are some promises I've been waiting on for over thirty years. I think to myself, "How can I be pregnant for this long? It's so uncomfortable!" But God knows what He's doing. He knows when to fulfil His promises. But there are some conditions to seeing the manifestation of these promises.

God calls us to be fruitful, and fruitfulness flows out of intimacy. We have to be yielded to God, full of His Spirit, and listening to His heart.

Look at the amazing story told in Luke chapter 1:

"In the sixth month of Elizabeth's pregnancy, God sent the angel Gabriel to Nazareth, to a town in Galilee, to a virgin pledged to be married to a man named Joseph, a descendent of David. And the virgin's name was Mary. And the angel went to her and

said, 'Greetings you who are highly favored! The Lord is with you.' Mary was greatly troubled at His words..."

Look at Mary. She's not married. She's around fourteen year's old. Now she has to tell her parents that she's seen an angel and she's pregnant! Who wouldn't be troubled? Who's going to believe this girl? I have had some wild promises from God, but this is mind-blowing. Yet, despite her circumstances and great personal cost, Mary accepted the promise and God's wondrous plan unfolded.

God has placed promises in your heart. There's not a single person reading this who hasn't been given a promise. There's not a single person reading who hasn't been predestined for fruitfulness. Read John 15. It says that you will have supernatural fruitfulness if you are connected to the vine, fully connected to Jesus.

The things God might speak to you could be bizarre. They could be things that you don't understand at all. (And if you could produce them on your own, by your own effort, I would have to say they're probably not the supernatural promises of God for your life anyway). Maybe they haven't come to pass yet? Maybe it all feels too hard? Maybe it seems too long to wait?

Don't give up! God wants you to carry His promises to "full term". He is asking you to come into that place of intimacy with Him, His secret place, where He can help and guide you.

Yield yourself to the One who is altogether beautiful and see what unfolds.

Day Twenty-One
Overshadowed

"Lord Almighty, blessed is the one who trusts in You."

(Psalm 84:12)

Mary's story is crazy. Not only is she going to have a baby, but He is going to be the Son of God who will have a Kingdom that will go on forever and ever.

I often have people say to me, "Why don't you get a plan together and do something manageable? Get a staff and train them well. And before you do anything, set a budget and raise some money to support your vision."

That sounds nice, but if we have everything all figured out, what room is there for utter dependence on our Father God? What room is there for miraculous, supernatural intervention that brings glory to Jesus?

Twenty-seven years ago, we went to Indonesia with a one-way ticket and thirty dollars in our pocket. Of course, people said, "You can't do that!" We soon had no money at all and it was hard, but I know that if we'd waited until we had everything together, all nicely planned out and paid for, we never would have gone anywhere! We'd still be sitting there, waiting for something to happen. The fact is, when you are intimate with God, then you are totally yielded to Him. And He can do anything through yielded vessels who carry His love.

Think of Mary. We have a lot of kids around us the whole time. If one showed up and told me a story about an angel appearing, telling her she was going to have a baby, I'd think, "Uh, huh. Good try!" God didn't make it easy for Mary. He didn't say, "The logical way to do this is for you to get married first, so let's plan the wedding and have a party. Then you can become pregnant and have the baby. That will look better."

Of course, He didn't do that. What He asked Mary to do was dangerous and costly. She could have been ridiculed or, worse, made an outcast, rejected by Joseph and her family. Knowing this, Mary still yielded. She said, "Yes!" to being completely inconvenienced, completely taken over. She didn't really understand anything that was happening, but she was in love with God and trusted Him with a simple, absolute trust. Her only question was a practical one:

"'How will this be,' Mary asked the angel. 'Since I am a virgin?' The angel answered, 'The Holy Spirit will come upon you, and the power of the most High will overshadow you. So the Holy One to be born will be called the Son of God.'" (Luke 1:34-35)

The Lord Himself wants to overshadow *you*. He wants to be so intimate with you, so close to you, so filling you, that whatever He says, you will want to do.

Let your simple, trusting prayer today be, "I don't understand, but go ahead, Lord, overshadow me." That simple prayer will lead you on an amazing journey.

Day Twenty-Two
Persevere

"You need to persevere so that when you have done the will of God, you will receive what He has promised."

(Hebrews 10:36)

The enemy always tries to kill a promise before it hits full term. He will do anything to try and make you lose heart and give up.

Carrying a promise is hard. Maybe you're thinking, "This is too much for me. I do not want to 'show' what I'm carrying. I do not want to carry this. It's uncomfortable and too painful. And surely you don't expect me to carry it past a year? Two years? *Five* years?"

Maybe you're full of promises that never happened? Did you sense God promise that signs and wonders would break forth in your city? Or that you would start a church? Or see a healing revival? Maybe He gave you a vision ten years ago and it started well but has slowly fizzled out? Are you reading this thinking you've heard promises for so long that you're sick and tired of hearing them and you don't want another prophecy because your bags are already full?

The temptation is to let it go. You want to heave a sigh, shoulder the embarrassment, and walk away. But if we want to see supernatural fruitfulness, we have to persevere. No matter how odd we may look, we mustn't give up. We have to carry the promise to full term. We have to be prepared to be heavy with our promise, whatever people think. We have to be stretched, inconvenienced, blown out of all proportion; to waddle around and wait and wait…

Because it's worth it.

When God called me to care for every dying child that He put in front of me each day, He said, "Take them all, that Father's house may be full."

I said, "Well, Lord, that's wonderful and I'll do it – I'll never say no to a dying child. But, but, but Lord… Isn't that a bit too much for little old me?"

He said, "It's *really* a lot for you. But it's not a lot for Me."

I said, "But I can't understand how I'll do it."

He said, "You won't understand it. But I'll place a love inside of you that will grow and grow and grow. And for the joy set before you, you'll endure."

Now, every time I get to a new place and God challenges me to take more children I say, "But…but… but…Yes!"

Guess what though? Even though Father has ripped the "no" out of me, the enemy *still* tries to kill the promise.

When our ministry began, people ridiculed us. Family and friends didn't understand. Newspapers called us everything under the sun: child traffickers, sellers of children's body parts, drug dealers, counter-revolutionaries, leaders of a drunken cult. We've been written up for *everything*. I've been thrown in jail twice and been held under house arrest.

Even today, not much has changed. Every time we move forward, something happens that tries to make us give up. The enemy is constantly trying to cut the umbilical cord of the growing promise. But the Lord is asking us to persevere, to carry the promise to full term.

In Portuguese, the words for giving birth are *dar a luz*, which essentially means to "bring light". It's a beautiful image. Today God says to you, "Don't give up before you give birth. Don't give up! Wait and bring the light of the promise I have given you to a dying world."

Ask Abba Daddy to show you who you are. Look into His eyes and know you are His. You are not an orphan, you are beloved and chosen. You are legally adopted and through Christ Jesus you have access to healing, wisdom and provision... to everything that Jesus has!

Day Twenty-Three
Shine

*"Praise be to the God and Father of our Lord Jesus Christ,
who has blessed us in the heavenly realms with every spiritual
blessing in Christ."*

(Ephesians 1:3)

The verse above confirms that God *has* blessed us. God has
blessed *you*. He's not hoping to bless you. He's not going to
bless you if you pray enough. He *has* blessed you with *every*
spiritual blessing. Wow! If you will just believe this, not just
with your head, but with your heart, then you will begin to live
in a totally different way.

Even though you may get up each day and do normal things
like brushing your teeth, washing, going to work, you are
not called to live in this natural realm. Your life has been
transferred to another dimension! In truth, you are living in
heavenly realms with Christ, and everything you have comes
from Jesus.

One day I had been preaching at a conference and after it
finished, I rushed to catch a plane. I was absolutely exhausted

but, to my delight, I found I had been upgraded to first class. It was the best of the best seats – so snazzy! I got a pillow and even pajamas! I was so happy, I was beaming with delight and all the other people were looking at me oddly. I kept saying, "Thank you so much, this is amazing. Thank you, thank you!" I was so enthusiastic.

Finally, a lady came over to me and said, "*Who are you?* Everybody's talking about you. You're so different."

I said, "I love Jesus! I'm a minister of the Gospel."

She said, "We knew it! You were glowing when you got on the plane and we knew something was different. Where are you preaching? How can we get there?"

I didn't have to preach with words. I preached with my smile. I preached with eye-contact.

As ambassadors for Jesus on this earth, we must be living sacrifices, filled to the brim and overflowing with His kindness, mercy, gentleness, meekness and appreciation. But I'll act exactly the same if I'm with the lost, the poor or lepers.

God takes us from this realm and places us in another realm. He creates us to shine. When you know who you are and what you carry within you, *you just glow with it*. It doesn't matter if you're sitting with a beggar on the street or next to a President – you treat everyone with the same love and respect God does.

Make sure you know what you carry within you and let the presence of Christ shine out, wherever you are and whoever you are with!

Day Twenty-Four
Adopted

"He chose us in Him before the creation of the world to be holy and blameless in His sight. In love He predestined us for adoption to sonship through Jesus Christ, in accordance with His pleasure and will."

(Ephesians 1:4-5)

When God looks at you, He's excited. He chose you and He's actually happy about you being His. He adopted you. When you know exactly who you are, it brings a supernatural rest.

Exodus 33:14 says, *"My presence will go with you, and I will give you rest."* This isn't a rest from doing anything, it describes the utter sense of peace that comes from knowing you belong and are accepted.

However, many of us do not walk in this supernatural peace and rest. We struggle with our identity and still act as if we're orphans. I know from experience that orphans have a completely different mentality! Orphans worry about being loved. They think they have to fight for favor and attention. They feel overlooked, so they jostle for position or push themselves forwards. They tear others down and are competitive and critical.

But when an orphan knows who they are – that they are loved – everything changes. They change in the way they treat themselves and they change in the way they treat others. Suddenly their hopes and dreams are able to burst forth and blossom.

In the same way, it is vital that we truly understand who we are in Christ. We are His representatives on the earth and, before we start to work for Him, we must be certain of our identity. If we're not, we won't be able to fearlessly and spontaneously act when He calls us   . We won't trust that He's with us. We won't depend on His power. We'll get tired and burnt out and all anyone will see will be a miserable, fearful Christian living in the natural realm. No one will see the beauty of Christ and His ways.

Philippians 2:5 says. *"In your relationships with one another, have the same mindset as Christ Jesus."*

We are to look like Him, talk like Him, walk like Him, love like Him, do miracles like Him, heal like Him. All of this comes from understanding who we are in Christ. The more we know who we are, the more we will boldly believe that God can do anything, with anyone.

Ask Abba Daddy to show you who you are. Look into His eyes and know you are His. You are not an orphan, you are beloved and chosen. You are legally adopted and through Christ Jesus you have access to healing, wisdom and provision… to everything that Jesus has!

Day Twenty-Five
He Knows You!

"Before I formed you in the womb I knew you, before you were born I set you apart..."

(Jeremiah 1:5)

Most people pick and choose the things they think God could use in them. And it's always their strengths, their likes, their passions. But God knows everything and uses everything.

Genesis 50:20 (MSG) says, *"Don't you see, you planned evil against me but God used those same plans for my good."*

When we started out in ministry, God specifically told me to only have one outfit to wear and one to wash, and to only eat what the poor would eat. Even though I was raised in a way where I understood how to eat and dress properly, I was totally happy to lay all that aside and go and live amongst the very poor.

But God knew my history. He knew my parents. He knew that I would one day have to sit with Presidents and eat with sterling silver and crystal. He knew that that's what had been drilled into me: how to sit, how to eat, how to talk, what to do. Even though I left that world and went to the slums, I had inside of me that thing I would need for the future.

God knows who you are. God knows where you were born. He knows your culture. He knows you! There's nothing in your life that He won't use for His glory. Paul wrote, *"...all things work for the good of those who love Him"* (Romans 8:28)

Because God created your personality, He's not about to push you into stuff you won't like. Instead, He works on your heart to soften it and make it pliable. There are parts of you that God knows about and you don't! You may think you're called to be a missionary, but God knows you should be a bank manager. Or vice versa. You may think, "Can I bend that far?" Yes, you can!

I fought God when He spoke to me about reaching other nations, and reaching the government in Mozambique. I told Him, "That's not who I am. That's not what I like. It's not what I want!" He worked on me to soften my heart until eventually I just said yes.

Recently, I was getting ready to head into a village to pray with the poor. I was going to sit with those who were sick and also visit my friends. I love doing that. In fact, I adore it. Just as I was about to go, I got a message saying that the Minister of Education had turned up at our school and I needed to go and meet with him. The meeting took all of my time, so I didn't get to go to the village. I'm OK with this because my life is not my own.

When we tell God who we are and what we can do, we're not pliable in His hands. He can't use us the way He wants to. But if we surrender to Him, everything will turn out for the good!

Jeremiah 29:11 says. *"For I know the plans I have for you, declares the Lord, plans to prosper you and not to harm you, plans to give you hope and a future."*

Today, give Him everything. He knows who you are. He knows what you're for. Trust Him.

Day Twenty-Six
The Mind of Christ

"I keep asking that the God of our Lord Jesus Christ, the glorious Father, may give you the Spirit of wisdom and revelation, so that you may know Him better."

(Ephesians 1:17)

Many people are seeking answers to different issues in their life. Some are struggling with issues and anxieties that keep them awake at night. Others have problems that they just can't seem to figure out. Instead of worrying about these things or trying to use our brains to figure out the answers, we need to step into that intimate place with God and ask the Lord to speak to us. He'll give us His wisdom, His revelation and His knowledge. Every single day.

James 1:5 tells us that, *"If any of you lacks wisdom, you should ask God, who gives generously to all without finding fault, and it will be given to you."*

God is faithful. When we hide ourselves in His secret place, His wisdom will hit us. The Word says it *will* be given, not that *it might* be given. Wisdom helps us see things the way God does. Revelation reveals things we did not know.

Paul explains in Ephesians 1:22 that, *"God placed all things under His [Jesus] feet and appointed Him to be head over everything for the church, which is His body, the fullness of Him who fills everything in every way."*

This should blow us away, because it's incredible! Paul is telling us that Jesus is "the head" and we are "the body". It's like Jesus is the *mind* of the Church, and He fills us up with Himself, if we are yielded to Him. Elsewhere, in 1 Corinthians 2:16 Paul confirms that as followers of Jesus, *"We have the mind of Christ."* This is so powerful.

Try this. Put your hand on your head and say, "I receive the mind of Christ. I receive the wisdom and revelation of Christ. You who fill everything, fill me in every way. Yes, Lord!"

We are the body of Jesus. We are the hands, the feet, the mouth, the heart. Jesus wants to take us, fill us up, and send us out.

As the body of Christ, each one of us has to say "Yes" to Jesus' call and empty ourselves of "us", so that He can flow through us more fully. The more we pour ourselves out, the more Holy Spirit can pour His love, wisdom and revelation in.

Pray with me: "Lord, I am your possession. I want you to find joy in my life. I want to be available. I want to make you smile. I'm willing to go anywhere, say anything, do anything for You. I thank you that You will give me the wisdom, revelation and knowledge to do it when I ask. Amen."

Day Twenty-Seven
Willing to Die?

"You are the light of the world. A town built on a hill cannot be hidden. Neither do people light a lamp and put it under a bowl. Instead they put it on its stand, and it gives light to everyone in the house. In the same way, let your light shine before others, that they may see your good deeds and glorify your Father in heaven."

(Matthew 5:14-16)

Many people are casual about their faith. There's no conviction of sin, no repentance. But when Peter witnessed the incredible miracle of Jesus, filling his boat so full of fish that it started to sink, he was so overpowered by the presence of God that he couldn't stand it.

"When Simon Peter saw this, he fell at Jesus' knees and said, 'Go away from me Lord for I am a sinful man!'" (Luke 5:8)

The all-mighty, all-powerful presence of God is tangible, terrible and convicting, yet the Church seems to have watered it down. It wants short-cuts. Short-cuts into His presence, short-cuts to His power, short-cuts to His mighty Kingdom.

But the Christian life is not a casual thing. We're in a ferocious battle. Good against evil, angels against demons. This is a battle for life or death. A battle for eternity. Everything we say and do has eternal consequences and huge significance. That's why it says in Proverbs 1:7, *"The fear of the Lord is the beginning of wisdom."*

We will never appreciate salvation and grace, being in that perfect place of love (where there is no fear) until we start with the fear of the Lord and realize exactly what we've been saved from.

I met Canon Andrew White, whose church is located right in the heart of the warzone in Baghdad, Iraq. He is known as the Vicar of Baghdad. He has lots of former terrorists in his church who have found Christ. Countless members of that congregation have died for their faith in Jesus. When people convert from other religions to Christianity, they are not thinking about all the leadership conferences or worship events they will attend. They know they are likely sacrificing this life for the next. It's that simple. They have accepted Jesus as their Savior and believe that the Bible is the truth – and they are staking their lives on it.

Matthew 16:25 (AMP) says, *"For whoever wishes to save his life (in this world) will (eventually) lose it (through death), but whoever loses his life (in this world) for My sake will find it (that is, life with Me for all eternity)."*

In most of the world there is persecution. In most of the world Christians do not have the freedom those in the West have. The question for them is a very simple one: *is Jesus worth it?* It really is about giving up the greatest temptations Satan can throw at you and placing all your faith in God.

How much do *we* demonstrate our choice in this life? Is it visible? Do *our* lives display how much we love and trust your God? Are you casual about your faith? Every action, every word should reflect your choice. But does it? It's challenging isn't it?

Day Twenty-Eight
A Powerful Crop

"Thy Kingdom come, thy will be done on earth, as it is in heaven."

(Matthew 6:10)

Let's think about what "kingdom" means. A kingdom has to have a King. A King who rules. What the King purposes, happens. And God has a purpose for this world and our life in it.

As followers of Jesus we are caught up in a massive showdown between good and evil and we must never forget that. Job is a good example of this.

In Job 1:9-12 we read about the accuser highlighting Job to God as an example. He says, "Oh, he doesn't love You. You've put a hedge around him and blessed him in every way. How do you know he really loves you? How do you know what's really in his heart? How do you know he hasn't just married you for your money?"

Job then went through a terrible time of testing, but he stood firm in his faith.

Why? Because he was properly rooted in relationship with God.

It's a sad fact that many people give up on God as soon as they don't get the answers they want to their prayers. They get angry when they can't get God to do what they want. They grumble and complain for a few years, then after a while they just drift off.

The parable of the sower illustrates this well

"A farmer went out to sow his seed. As he was scattering the seed, some fell along the path, and the birds came and ate it up. Some fell on rocky places, where it did not have much soil. It sprang up quickly, because the soil was shallow. But when the sun came up, the plants were scorched, and they withered because they had no root. Other seed fell among thorns, which grew up and choked the plants. Still other seed fell on good soil, where it produced a crop—a hundred, sixty or thirty times what was sown." (Matthew 13:4-9)

We see that there are four different types of seed scattered, but only one portion of seed produced a crop. The quality of the soil determined the quality of the crop – just like Job.

Love and devotion toward God. Taking time to listen to Him in the secret place of His heart. Yielding to His will. Perseverance and surrender. All of these form "good soil" in a life – soil that is ready to receive His seed, protect it, and allow it to grow.

This kind of relationship with our Father God produces a crop of love, joy, peace, patience, kindness, goodness, faithfulness, gentleness and self-control, all of which spring up.

Let's put down our will and surrender to God's will for us. Let's become living sacrifices for Him, seeking how we can bless Him rather than how He can bless us. Let's be planted in good soil and yield a powerful crop.

Day Twenty-Nine
Finding God

"You will seek me and find me when you seek me with all your heart."

(Jeremiah 29:13)

I think the Bible tells us to "seek God with all our hearts" because most of us seek Him with our heads! We have a theological idea of who He is, or a vague belief system, or we might go on a study course that teaches *about* Him... But Jeremiah tells us quite clearly that we won't find Him that way. The only way we will find God is if we have an actual, living relationship with him. This demands dialogue, intimacy and love.

Deuteronomy 6:5 makes this abundantly clear: *"Love the Lord your God with all your heart and with all your mind and with all your soul and with all your strength."*

I believe that the real question of the Christian life is not how to accomplish the Great Commission and make our churches full. The real question is: *How do I relate to God? How do I find Him and engage with Him?*

If we are honest, most of us don't really know Him very well at all. If we did, we'd know that He is fun and childlike, interesting and emotional. He's more of a friend. He's interested in the details of our lives. He's deeply involved in our everyday. He's not a distant God, but a close companion.

When we seek Him with all our heart, we'll be totally swept away by Him. We'll want to spend time with Him. We'll want to know what He thinks and want to do what He says. We'll not be afraid to give Him our hopes and dreams and to hand Him the responsibility for our lives.

And there's no limit to how close you can get to God. Some churches act as if God is far away. They pray vague prayers in a solemn tone, as if He is sitting up in heaven, barely listening. But that's not true! Finding God, relating to Him, living with Him is *the most important* thing. You can be a monk in a monastery and pray for thirty years and barely know God. You can have huge success, a massive church, mission work and miracles, but they mean nothing without a close relationship with the One who is Love.

1 Corinthians 13:2 says, *"If I have the gift of prophecy and can fathom all mysteries and all knowledge, and if I have a faith that can move mountains, but do not have love, I am nothing."*

We can't do anything by ourselves – only through a powerful, intimate relationship with Jesus. Satan's whole agenda is to prevent this relationship. He strives to make us fix our minds on temporal, earthly things, rather than on things above. He tempts us with things we can see, things we can do, things we want – anything to distract us from God. It's a constant battle, so be careful. Guard your hearts. The enemy will use anything to draw you away from God and his ways can be subtle.

We are called to live in the spiritual realm. We are spiritual beings, deep in enemy territory. Let's seek God, find Him and know Him. Let's be single-minded in our desire to know Him fully. That's what will bring us joy and peace, and lead to an outpouring that will change the world.

Day Thirty
Fire

"John answered them all, 'I baptize you with water. But one who is more powerful than I will come, the straps of whose sandals I am not worthy to untie. He will baptize you with the Holy Spirit and fire."

(Luke 3:16)

How many of you would like to be so thrilled with God and what He asks of you that you're totally happy? Blissfully happy? So happy that it bursts out of you in uncontrollable joy?

Church is weird because you come in, sit down, and listen a lot. But when you're fully yielded to God, so full of His love, you actually want to laugh and jump and dance and sing. Do you think you'll come into heaven and sit quietly in a pew?

1 Peter 1:8 says, *"Though you have not seen him, you love Him, and even though you do not see Him now, you believe in Him and are filled with an inexpressible and glorious joy."*

One thing I've discovered about God is that He really dislikes being stopped. Many pastors and leaders fall into the trap of running their meetings despite God, rather than for Him. They are nervous about things getting "out of hand", so anything that seems weird or out of the ordinary is quickly shut down. Obviously, those who are attention seeking or creating a demonic distraction need to be spiritually discerned and dealt with – but often it is the people who are desperately hungry for God who let loose in unconventional ways. They are not trying to be weird, it's just that their hunger has surpassed their fear of what others might think. Their eyes are fixed on Jesus.

Such hungry people are often those who Father God uses as kindling for the great fires that are about to burst out. No revival ever got started by shutting everything down! Revivals have always been started by rebels. By people who are so on fire for God that you can't hold them down. You can't put out the flames. Sparks fly off them and set people alight. Then it gets hotter and hotter and kindles a huge fire that spreads outwards. Red hot kindling starts fires!

We want those revival fires, don't we? A huge hunger for God that spreads throughout our communities. We can't save people by shouting at them, arguing with them or criticizing their way of life. They have to see and feel the difference in us. They have to be drawn by the warmth and wonder of the fire, captivated by Holy Spirit flames.

Our biggest aim shouldn't be to start a revival, but to kindle our own personal revival. To stoke our fires until sparks fly and others are set alight. Very soon, a great fire *will* burn and its heat will spread from church to church, town to town, until holy fires are breaking out across the world.

Day Thirty-One
Only Jesus

"I keep my eyes always on the Lord. With Him at my right hand, I will not be shaken."

(Psalm 16:8)

The Bible tells us that the disciples preached the Gospel *first*, then confirmed the word with signs and wonders *following* (Mark 16:20).

Some people are frustrated by this. They want manifestations and healings and deliverances, without any foundation in the wisdom and knowledge of Jesus.

There have been massive healing crusades in Africa and other countries, but this doesn't necessarily grow the Church or lead people into a long term relationship with Jesus. Yet, that is what we want. Without that, there won't be much fruit. It's a solid marriage we want, not just some fun for a while.

I have discovered through experience that the human tendency is to get caught up with the miracles and manifestations. They become the focus, rather than Jesus. I know people who go from one signs and wonders meeting to the next. They need that atmosphere, that excitement. But in between they are dry, unstable, cranky, desperate and lost. It's like an addiction.

Supernatural manifestations don't love you. They don't talk to you. They're an experience that God gives you, but they're not Him. They don't mean anything unless you know Him. Set your heart on Jesus and appreciate the manifestations; not the other way around.

Joy, laughter, healing and miracles are the outcome of the Gospel. They're the *end* result, not the beginning.

Romans 14:17 teaches, *"The Kingdom of God is not meat and drink; but righteousness, and peace, and joy in the Holy Spirit."* There's a reason that God puts it in that order.

I was born in China and grew up there. There were Buddhist temples everywhere, filled with incense, gold and idols, and the monks with their rituals and prayer wheels. There were demons everywhere and that's why, when I get into high sacramental churches that are full of images and gold and incense, it reminds me of those temples. Everything *around* Jesus is being worshipped, but this can be a distraction; a fuzzy cloud that makes a true heart-on-heart meeting really difficult.

Paul said in 2 Corinthians 11:3 (AMP) *"But I am afraid that... your minds may be corrupted and led away from the simplicity of (your sincere and) pure devotion to Christ."*

Pure devotion to Christ is all that matters. It's Jesus. He's the point. Only Jesus. He's the answer to everything.

Colossians 1:15 tells us that, *"The Son is the perfect image of the invisible God."*

Whatever your question is, whatever your need is, whatever your crisis is, there's only one answer: Jesus.

Day Thirty-Two
Cast Your Crown

"...where the spirit of the Lord is, there is freedom."

(2 Corinthians 3:17)

A while ago we decided to write a mission statement for Iris Global to help people understand exactly what it is that we do. So, I did a bit of research and I noticed that almost all mission statements start by saying: Our mission is to save the lost, fulfil the Great Commission, feed the poor, clothe the widow, transform the world, love the unlovely, disciple the nations...

All this sounds good, doesn't it? And it is good! But it struck me that all these mission statements are about the stuff *we do for God*, rather than about our relationship with Him. I want to ask you: what is our primary calling? What is the most important thing that the Bible tells us to do?

Love.

In Matthew 22:37 Jesus distilled the commands of God to their essence in this beautifully simple way:

"Jesus replied, 'Love the Lord your God with all your heart and with all your soul and with all your mind. This is the first and greatest commandment. And the second is like it: Love your neighbor as yourself.'"

Going out and doing mission is all well and good, but first we have to be rooted and grounded in love, in Christ, otherwise we're missing the whole point.

Paul spoke of this imperative in Ephesians 3:17-18:

"And I pray that you, being rooted and established in love, may have power, together with all the Lord's holy people, to grasp how wide and long and high and deep is the love of Christ."

We can go out on the mission field and perform miracles and do fascinating things, and this is amazing, but it's not personal. Our hearts are designed for love and intimacy; for relationship. That's what the Kingdom is made out of. To make the kingdom great we need to get close to the King.

We must bind ourselves to Him and His will, so that we know what to do in life. Knowing what He wants us to do will satisfy us and make us happier than we could ever be going our own way. God can put so much freedom and joy into you if He gets His way. When the Holy Spirit is fully in control of you, that is when you are most happy.

Isaiah 55:9 tells us, *"As the heavens are higher than the earth, so are My ways higher than your ways and My thoughts than your thoughts."*

Our Father knows best. God's ways make us happier than our ways. When God asked us to move to the slums and give away all our stuff, it filled us with joy. It was a privilege!

He knows us better than we know ourselves. Life is thrilling and we see great fruit because God is active. He's pouring Himself into us, making us holy, transforming us through His beauty and love. We can't do it ourselves. He's the Master Sculptor. He's taking our lives and making something beautiful from them. We are His workmanship.

Come to God with empty hands and total humility and ask Him to fill you. Then love Him with all your heart, soul and mind and, when people give *you* glory for the miracles and manifestations that follow, cast your crown at His feet.

Day Thirty-Three
Delighting

*"Delight yourself in the Lord, and He will give you the desires of
your heart."*

(Psalm 37:4 AMP)

I always like to say that most people don't go to church because
they looked inside one once!

Think about it. If you cannot delight in the Lord, what's the
point of doing anything for Him? And what does God get out
of it? Having a lot of people suffering hardship for Him like
good soldiers of Christ is not the same as having a true, loving
relationship with just one of them.

I believe that most people don't experience any joy in their
walk with Jesus because their total focus is on the second part
of this verse.

How can we get God to give us the desires of our heart?

People want to know how to get a breakthrough. They key word
is *want*. What is it you want? We can usually think of plenty of
things we want and we try to figure out ways in which we can

get them. If we can't get them on our own, we invariably turn to God and ask Him to get them for us!

The problem is, we don't want God for who He is; we want Him for what He can do for us; for what He can give us. We begin reading books that might give us the answer, joining a different church, looking for clues as to how we can get the desires of our heart. We strive and beg and give money and pray, thinking it's what *we do* that will get us our breakthrough. All we want is God's power working for us.

How can we make our church grow? How can we get a new job? How can we pay off our debts? How can we find the right husband/wife?

We have a long list of stuff that we think will make us happy, yet we neglect the only person who *truly can*. I sometimes think that Jesus is the loneliest, most misunderstood, most unappreciated, most left-out person in the Church!

Think about your life. Aren't the most important things, that bring you the most joy, your relationships? In the end, it's not what you've achieved, the honors you've received or the blessings you've had that matter. It's the rich relationships of life. Parent/child, brother/sister, mother/father, friends…

This is what God wants with you and me. A deep, rich relationship of mutual love. We're made in His image and God wants to be wanted just as much as we do. He wants us to delight in Him… for Him.

Psalm 73:25 says, *"Whom have I in heaven but you? And earth has nothing I desire besides you."*

Next time you pray, come to Him with the intention of delighting in Him and nothing else. Come to Him as a little child wanting to press yourself into His arms to hear His heartbeat. Roll every care onto Him and then let go. He knows the desires of your heart, so trust Him with them.

Day Thirty-Four
Simple Love

"I have loved you with an everlasting love; I have drawn you with unfailing kindness."

(Jeremiah 31:3)

When I was at college, I was told that if I read the Bible and prayed for an hour every morning, my day would go well. So, I made myself get up early, got my stop-watch and made myself read the Bible. I made myself think of something to pray about, then charged out to see if the day went better.

It didn't.

Seeking God's face is not a discipline. It's not hard work. It's not a matter of filling a prayer slot. You wouldn't treat a good friend like that, would you? So why be like that with God? It's not very loving to set your watch in order to make sure you talk to your friend for a full ten minutes. It's not loving to agree, out of guilt, to fill a one-hour slot to hang out. It's not loving to crank out lifeless prayers at meetings. The world knows what love is and, when the world looks, they see religion rather than relationship.

As anyone knows who's fallen in love: it's a mystery. It's not a chore to be with the person you love. You can't fake it, you can't force it, you can't figure it out. You don't grit your teeth and force yourself, it just happens. It bubbles up from deep within. It's the most natural thing in the world and it grows from spending time with each other. The real discipline should be guarding that love. Guarding time together and guarding against the enemy.

Jesus says in John 10:10, *"The thief comes only to steal and kill and destroy; I have come that they may have life, and have it to the full."*

If you have that secret relationship with God, then you're totally OK. Wherever you are, whatever you're going through, He is with you. He has the answers and wants to help. When you're grafted into Him, His power and love can reach you.

"I am the vine; you are the branches. If you remain in Me and I in you, you will bear much fruit; apart from me you can do nothing." (John 15:5)

We don't produce the answers, we don't produce the fruit, He does. But the flow comes from knowing and spending time with Him, not rushing through a meditation or parroting the Lord's prayer. Decide today to simply love Him, to sit with Him and chat. Soon the answers to every trouble or concern will rise like sap and glide from the vine to the branches.

Day Thirty-Five
Step by Step

"...I do not concern myself with great matters or things too wonderful for me. But I have calmed and quieted myself, I am like a weaned child with it's mother; like a weaned child I am content."

(Psalm 131:1)

Isn't it amazing that children believe everything their parents say? That's exactly what makes God happy. When we just trust Him and believe Him. A kid cannot explain why he loves his mom and he does everything she says. He just does.

Jesus says in Matthew 18:3, *"Truly I tell you, unless you change and become like little children, you will never enter the kingdom of heaven."*

We keep coming back to this theme of childlikeness because it's so critical. The Kingdom is accessible to children. You can't get in unless you're a kid! It doesn't matter if you're a trained theologian or an expert in cultural/spiritual trends, or have a massive intellect or skill in some other area. You must be childlike.

Children are dependent on their parents. As such, they just trust and, much of the time, don't really know what's going on. Being childlike before God means being 100% dependent on Him speaking to you, leading you, helping you, and doing things through you.

A while ago we were out on a visit to a remote village. The villagers had asked for help to build a fence and a little prayer house, so Heidi asked one of our staff members to stay behind with them. This girl had absolutely no clue how they were going to do it. There were a few Mozambicans and herself – that was it! But people found wood, found other people who could help, and a fence got built. Then they made a nice little prayer house and decorated it.

Our staff member didn't know what she was doing, she just depended on God. Then they got bags of rice and presents and gave them out to the people there. Pretty soon the villagers fell in love with the team. Then some people started getting healed and more and more people came. Then Muslims started coming asking about Jesus…

The whole scenario just unfolded under God's direction and it didn't matter that this girl didn't know what she was doing. She hadn't known what would happen, who would offer help, who would ask questions or be healed. She didn't know anything! But God did.

We have a lot of experience in the mission field and we try to teach others what we know. We have made many mistakes and done so many dumb things but, by the grace of God, we're still here, and our ceiling is your floor! *But* it's all nothing without the leading of the Holy Spirit.

Without hearing God *specifically* for yourself in a given situation you cannot confidently walk forward. Don't rely on others, don't blindly follow. Ask Him yourself, "What do I do, Lord?" You actually don't need to know anything other than that.

Whatever you're dealing with today, look to your Father. Take it step by step. He might ask you to forgive someone, or speak to a stranger, or help build a fence... Who knows? But whatever He asks you to do, just do it!

Day Thirty-Six
A River Running Through You

"For I was hungry and you gave me something to eat. I was thirsty and you gave me something to drink, I was a stranger and you invited me in, I needed clothes and you clothed me, I was sick and you looked after me, I was in prison and you came to visit me."

(Matthew 25:35)

How do you love the invisible God? The verse above explains how.

That's huge. If you get really off track and disappear to a desert island to be spiritual for decades, you've missed the point. I think Jesus likes to be *physically* loved. How do we do that? By loving people.

God wants a real relationship with us, in which we spend time drinking in His beauty and filling up on love. *Then*, He wants us out there, loving people with that same beauty and love. It's a river running through us.

The problem comes when we stop the flow at one end or the other. If we disconnect from Jesus to go off and do "important church stuff", then the flow stops. We burn out or run on empty. If we let the flow in, but stop helping others, then it all becomes a self-satisfying overflow. Neither grows fruit or the Kingdom of God.

The persecuted Church in China taught me that prayer is like breathing: if you stop you die. You must always keep that connection.

Loving people isn't just about making a difference in their lives on earth or improving their situation – we're talking about their eternity. We're not just making someone's circumstances better, we're rescuing them from hell and getting them to heaven. It's pretty astounding isn't it?

Matthew 25:40 says, *"Truly I tell you, whatever you did for one of the least of these brothers and sisters of mine, you did for me."*

Let the river of God's love and beauty run through you today. Let it pour out over the sick, the broken, the poor, the lonely. For by loving others, you are truly loving God.

Day Thirty-Seven
Unquenchable Grace

*"When He saw the crowds, he had compassion on them,
because they were harassed and helpless, like sheep without a
shepherd."*

(Matthew 9:36)

One time Rolland and I were in South Africa and I was sick. I
was dying in the hospital with a flesh-eating viral disease and I'd
been in hospital for thirty-three days. The disease had started
in my legs and, at first, the doctors told me they wanted to
amputate my legs. What you need to know is, *I love to run.* So,
while I was lying there, I said to Rolland, "Go and buy me some
new running shoes. I'm going to need new running shoes."
He didn't question me – he knows me too well! However, the
disease was rapidly spreading into my organs and the doctors
said it was too late. They told me I was going to die.

Immediately God said to me, "Go to Toronto." So, I checked
myself out of the hospital. I told them, "I'm going to be seen by
a specialist, because you guys said you couldn't help me." The
nurses looked at me and smiled. They knew. Many of them had
come to me in the night and, even though I was weak, I had

prayed for them and led them to the Lord. But the doctors said I would die. With tears running down their faces they offered me a last ditch course of antibiotics that might prolong my life. They were called "compassion antibiotics". I thought that was wild. *Compassion* antibiotics! I was searching for mercy, and mercy and compassion go hand in hand. My spirit jumped because I knew it was prophetic.

I flew to Toronto and the church there said, "Please don't preach, please don't speak." I think they were worried I was going to die on their video! But I told them, "You don't understand. For thirty-three days God has been putting a message in my heart. I have to speak."

I remember crawling up to the pulpit. It was clear, like crystal, so I couldn't hide behind it. And I remember saying these words:

Zachariah 2:5 says, *"For I, declares the Lord, will be a wall of fire around about you, and I will be the glory within you."*

As soon as I said, "the glory within you", the mercy of God, merciful Jesus, hit me from my head to my toes three times. It felt as though "mercy" had just exploded within me. I was totally, completely and instantly healed. I started dancing. The next morning, I got up really early and I put on the new running shoes Rolland had bought for me. I went running for an hour with absolutely no pain and no weakness after thirty-three days in the hospital. Every wound was totally healed!

The Lord is merciful to us!

Remember how Jesus' felt in Matthew 14:14: *"When Jesus... saw a large crowd, he had compassion on them and healed their sick."*

If you are sick right now, if you have been suffering or struggling, look into the face of Jesus. See the compassion in His eyes and take heart. He is a merciful, loving God who knows your frailties and longs to comfort and heal you!

Day Thirty-Eight
Mercy Triumphs

"Blessed are the merciful; for they shall obtain mercy."

(Matthew 5:7)

While I was seriously ill in that South African hospital, we got a phone call from the building contractor who was overseeing a huge amount of building work for us at our mission base. He told us that he had finished the work and he wanted payment. We paid him, then flew on to Toronto.

When I flew home, totally healed, we found all the workers furious. They had rocks and sticks and there was a huge riot. We soon discovered that the contractor had fled the country with all the money! He hadn't paid any of the workers and had left us with a massive debt for unfinished buildings. Well what do you do with that?

I believe in mercy, so I cried out "Mercy!"

Matthew 5:7 says, *"Blessed are the merciful; for they shall obtain mercy."*

We needed mercy, so we had to be merciful.

I said, "I'm not going to press charges. Leave him." One of his contractors, Xavier, came to me shaking. He said the workers wanted to kill him. He hadn't stolen the money, but he was one of the overseers and part of the management team, so he was going to go to jail because his boss had stolen the money.

Then the lord said to me, "Pay the debt!" So we paid the bill all over again! We paid all of the workers. We got Xavier released from prison and they finished the building work.

Not long after this I received a phone call to tell me that one of my kids had got drunk, stolen a car, smashed it up, and was in jail. I was not happy. I love him, but I was not happy! We were away preaching at the time, so I couldn't get him out of jail and let me tell you, jails in Mozambique are not very sweet. You don't want to be in jail for long! What happened was: Xavier, who had received mercy, took his own money, went to the jail, and paid for the smashed car, got the kid out of jail and brought him home!

He had been shown mercy, and he showed mercy. He poured the mercy of God out on this boy and, through it, that boy finally understood that he was a true son. Halleluiah!

Mercy is powerful. It is a river that flows contrary to the world and contrary to our flesh. It pours out favor and blessing on those who don't deserve it. Isn't it wonderful? And the most glorious thing is that the more we release mercy to others, the more we can receive it for ourselves!

Day Thirty-Nine
Godly Power

"Who is it that overcomes the world? Only the one who believes that Jesus is the son of God."

(1 John 5:5)

In the film *The Son of God* there is a line that really caught my attention. "Because the people could *feel* His power..." In other words, the people followed and trusted in God because He had revealed His power to them.

People tend to be attached to the idea of God's power for the wrong reasons. They announce "signs ands wonders" conferences, suggesting you'll get the breakthrough of your life through the power of God. Send in your money, they cry, to release your faith!

I don't believe it glorifies God when we promote and sell His tremendous power. Imagine Jesus getting up on a high mountain and shouting, "Hey, look at me! I'm powerful, watch this!" and bolts of lightning shoot out of his fingers. "And if you think that was amazing... watch this!"

That's not how He used His power at all. Jesus never broadcast His power one bit. In fact, He was so understated that most people would have missed it. Remember the little boy handing over his lunch, the healing of the lepers – Jesus dealt with it in a matter of fact way. I tell our staff that the more understated the miracle, the better it is! Jesus would just walk along, people would crowd around Him, and He would heal them. He did it gently and beautifully, saying, "Go and sin no more." That was it. No drama. Sometimes He didn't say much at all, or He might quietly say, "You're healed."

Jesus didn't work Himself up into a fervor. He didn't instruct His disciples in public relations. He didn't do anything to promote Himself. Here is the most powerful person in the universe, who at the same time is the most humble.

During the early years of our ministry, it was not uncommon for people to walk up to one hundred miles through the dirt and mud to get to us – not because we were trumpeting what we were doing, but because they'd heard via word of mouth: *Jesus is in town. The Spirit of God is moving.* People didn't care who we were, about our network of churches or the history of Iris; they didn't care about our degrees or how much we'd studied: they just wanted to encounter Jesus.

When you believe and trust that God is in control, you understand that He is able to look after His own reputation. It's not our job to try to make God look good. Our job is to walk in the power of God through love. Paul says the only thing that counts is faith working through love. If we don't have God's sheer, raw power working through us, then we have nothing. There is no kingdom if the King has no power.

1Corinthians 4:20 confirms that, *"For the Kingdom of God is not a matter of talk but of power."*

What is it that makes Christians different? That they do good? That they have a good moral code? No! The difference is that the other religions have no power, but Christianity does. We can walk into a village of lepers and talk to them about the moral code of God, but if we want to see them healed, we'll need His power. We ourselves don't have the power, but through our faith we do.

Where does spiritual power come from? It begins with love. *"The only thing that counts is faith expressing itself through love"* (Galatians 5:6). Through love comes faith, and through faith comes the power – the power to heal the sick, raise the dead; power for anything!

If you want to experience the power of God and see lives transformed as a result, the journey begins in the secret place, close to God's heart. It is born out of His all-consuming love. When we are filled with His love to overflowing, then it will begin to flow out of us to others, and the end result will be His love-filled power, working through us.

Day Forty
Make God Happy

"And now these three remain: faith, hope and love. But the greatest of these is love."

(1 Corinthians 13:13)

Song of Songs is a beautiful love song in the middle of the Bible. But nowhere in it does it mention God! People have allegorized it, but I think it's simply a love story about a guy and a girl. However, what makes it important and significant is that it teaches us about the very nature of love.

Song of Songs 8:6-7 reads, *"Place me like a seal over your heart, for love is as strong as death, its jealousy as unyielding as the grave. It burns like blazing fire, like a mighty flame. Many waters cannot quench love; rivers cannot sweep it away. If I were to give all the wealth of one's house for love, it would be utterly scorned."*

However much you are persecuted, love cannot be taken away. It's the greatest thing there is. It is stronger than death and cannot be explained. It's the most awesome thing. In general, Christian teaching passes over the sheer romance of the Christian life. The suggestion is made that God doesn't need love because He's God and He's perfect. But there is something romantic about Him that exceeds every human experience. That's extraordinary isn't it?

Over the years I've listened to many ideas about why God created us. There are many spiritual theories that sound good. He created us for His glory... for the sake of His name... He created us to make Himself known as holy in the world... to show His power... to change the world... to rule the world...

But I think God created us for Himself. He created us because He wanted to be loved for Himself, not for everything He can do. He's a romantic and He wants a partner. He wants a bride. He wants companionship and friendship. We're made for *Him*, in His image, so just as we need to be loved and valued and want companionship, so does God!

Don't you *think* He wants our love? To be loved for Himself, not for everything He can do? Does that make sense? We always say that Jesus is the only one who satisfies... but what would satisfy God? What does His heart crave? It's us!

See how that changes everything? It's not just about *us* being blessed and *us* being loved... it's about God being blessed and loved too! Think about that when you sit with Him and talk to Him today. Whatever issues you are struggling with, think how you can make God happy today too!

About IRIS Global

Rolland and Heidi's roots

Heidi and I began Iris Global (previously Iris Ministries) in 1980, and have been missionaries since then. We were both ordained as ministers in 1985 after completing our BA and MA degrees at Vanguard University in southern California. I majored in Biblical Studies, and Heidi in Church Leadership. I am a third-generation missionary born in China, and raised in China, Hong Kong and Taiwan. I was greatly influenced by my grandfather, H. A. Baker, who wrote "Visions Beyond the Veil," an account of the extended visions of heaven and hell that children received in his remote orphanage in southwest China two generations ago.

"Blessed are the poor in spirit, for theirs is the kingdom of heaven."– Matthew 5:3

Heidi was powerfully called to the mission field at age sixteen when she was living on an Indian reservation in Mississippi as an American Field Service student. Several months after she was led to Jesus by a Navajo evangelist, she was taken up in a vision for several hours and heard Jesus speak audibly to her and tell her to be a minister and a missionary to Asia, England and Africa. When she returned home to Laguna Beach, California, she began ministering at every opportunity and leading short-term missions teams. We met at a small charismatic church in Dana Point, and got married six months later after realizing we had the same radical desire to see revival among the poor and forgotten of the world.

Work in Asia and London

We spent our first six years together leading evangelistic dance-drama teams all over Asia, making use of our backgrounds in creative media and the performing arts. But we increasingly came into intimate contact with the desperately poor, and could no longer be satisfied by large meetings and quick visits to various locations, even though thousands were coming to Jesus. We had to learn to come to a stop and take care of long-term needs, one person at a time.

We began by working with the poor in the slums of central Jakarta, Indonesia, and then among the forgotten street-sleepers and elderly in the most crowded urban area in the world, central Kowloon in Hong Kong. Jackie Pullinger's work among drug addicts in the Walled City was a major influence in our lives.

In 1992 we left Asia to do our PhDs in systematic theology at King's College, University of London. But we couldn't stop ministering to the poor, and so at the same time we planted a warm and thriving church community for the homeless of downtown London, joined by a kaleidescope of students, lawyers, business people and friends from many countries. We learned the composite beauty of the Body of Christ!

Mozambique

For years we longed to get to Africa in fulfillment of our calling to prove the Gospel in the most challenging situation we could find. We wanted to see a continuation of "Visions Beyond the Veil," and believed with my grandfather that the most likely place to see such revival again was among the most unlikely! So we were drawn to Mozambique, officially listed at the time as the poorest country in the world.

A few days into my initial visit to Maputo, Mozambique's capital, I was offered an orphanage that no one could or would support, not even large churches in South Africa or European donor nations. It was horribly neglected and dilapidated, with eighty miserable, demon-afflicted orphans in rags. I thought it was a perfect test of the Sermon on the Mount. Our Father in heaven knows what we need. Seek first His Kingdom and righteousness, and these things will be ours as well … Take no thought for tomorrow. Why worry? Jesus is enough for us, for anyone.

Alone and without support, Heidi and I offered to take over the center and provide for the children in return for the opportunity to bring the Gospel to them. Within months the children were saved and filled with the Holy Spirit, weeping while still in rags with gratitude for their salvation. Jesus provided miraculously, more all the time as our children prayed night and day for their daily food. We brought in teams, improved the center, and took our children to the streets to testify to more orphaned and abandoned children. Some were lost in visions, taken to heaven and dancing around the throne of God on the shoulders of angels.

But abruptly, after we got up to 320 children, the government evicted us and denied our children permission to pray and worship on our property. Totally without a back-up plan, our children marched off the property barefoot without a home. We lost everything. We also lost tremendous amounts of support because we welcomed the increasing Presence of the Holy Spirit in our meetings.

But we were only beginning to taste the power of God in Mozambique. Land was donated by a nearby city. We got tents and food from South Africa. Provision came in from supernaturally touched hearts all over the world. Soon we could actually build our own dorms. Bush pastors longed for a Bible school, and to receive what our children had received from the Holy Spirit. Graduates went out and began healing the sick and raising the dead. Church growth in the bush exploded.

Then revival was fueled exponentially by the desperation caused by catastrophic flooding in 2000 when three cyclones came together and brought torrential rain for forty days and nights. More damage was caused by that flood than Mozambique's many years of civil war. A cry for God rose up like we had never experienced or imagined, and our churches across the country multiplied into thousands. God provided a bush airplane, which we used constantly to spread the Gospel through remote "bush conferences" at dirt airstrips in every province.

Expansion in Mozambique

There are networks of churches and church-based orphan care in all ten provinces in Mozambique in addition to bases in main cities. In recent years we have personally concentrated on the Makua, a people group in the north who were listed by missiologists as nearly unreached. With tremendous help from missionaries and nationals, since 2002, over two thousand churches have been planted among these people.

Each year thousands of visitors come to help us at our various bases, and we have a missions school in Pemba that offers something special to us: missions training on the mission field! Here we combine teaching, worship and spiritual impartation with everyday application to ministry among children and the poorest of the poor, both in towns and in the remote villages of the African bush.

IRIS Worldwide

Iris has over 35 bases in about 20 nations led by teams of missionaries and local leaders. As more and more people want to associate with us spiritually and in every way possible, our Iris family is expanding country by country, a step at a time. Bases are being established, works are being initiated, and in developed nations fervent believers wanting to participate with us in the Gospel are starting Iris charities. We welcome short-term and long-term applicants, and stress that Iris is a holistic ministry not limited to particular specialties. It includes evangelism, Bible schools, medical clinics, primary and secondary schools, farming, vocational training, church planting, bush conferences, counseling, child sponsorship and in the future, a university in Pemba for the poor! We make ourselves available to the Holy Spirit to make use of every gifting He brings our way. We celebrate the life of God among us in all its variety!

We are deeply encouraged by the fervent interest in ministry to the poor that we have encountered all over the world. We would like all those who want to work with us in some way to familarize themselves with our history, teaching and core values. A good place to start is our first book, *There is Always Enough*, detailing much of the story of how we got to this point. Another must on my short list is my grandfather's book, *Visions Beyond the Veil*, which is available on our website. For core values, read our 8 September 2010 newsletter. Use our Contact Form to make requests and ask questions. Much to follow, as the Lord wills…

In summary, we value immediate intimacy with Jesus, a life of utterly-needed miracles, concentration on the humble and lowly, willingness to suffer for love's sake, and the unquenchable joy of the Lord, which is our energy, motivation, weapon and reward — not optional!